Let's Fly

ROCKETS

by Wendy Hinote Lanier

FOCUS
READERS

www.focusreaders.com

Focus Readers is distributed by North Star Editions:
sales@northstareditions.com | 888-417-0195

Produced for Focus Readers by Red Line Editorial.

Photographs ©: Vera Larina/Shutterstock Images, cover, 1; Kim Shiflett/KSC/NASA, 4–5, 7, 19, 22–23; NASA Goddard/GSFC/NASA, 8–9; MSFC/NASA, 10, 14–15; Kenny Allen/JSC/NASA, 13, 29; Nostalgia for Infinity/Shutterstock Images, 17; Mikhail Starodubov/Shutterstock Images, 20–21; Owen Humphreys/PA Wire URN:34239335/AP Images, 25; Robert Markowitz/JSC/NASA, 26

Library of Congress Cataloging-in-Publication Data
Names: Lanier, Wendy Hinote, author.
Title: Rockets / by Wendy Hinote Lanier.
Description: Lake Elmo, MN : Focus Readers, [2019] | Series: Let's fly |
  Audience: Grades 4 to 6. | Includes bibliographical references and index.
  | Identifiers: LCCN 2018030732 (print) | LCCN 2018032082 (ebook) | ISBN
  9781641855150 (PDF) | ISBN 9781641854573 (e-book) | ISBN 9781641853415
  (hardcover) | ISBN 9781641853996 (pbk.)
Subjects: LCSH: Rockets (Aeronautics)--Juvenile literature. | Rocket
  engines--Juvenile literature. | Outer space--Exploration--Juvenile
  literature.
Classification: LCC TL782.5 (ebook) | LCC TL782.5 .L285 2019 (print) | DDC
  629.47--dc23
LC record available at https://lccn.loc.gov/2018030732

Printed in the United States of America
Mankato, MN
October, 2018

About the Author

Wendy Hinote Lanier is a native Texan and former elementary teacher who writes and speaks for children and adults on a variety of topics. She is the author of more than 30 books for children and young adults.

TABLE OF CONTENTS

CHAPTER 1

BLASTING OFF

A giant rocket sits on the launch pad. It is about to blast off. The rocket is 23 stories tall. It is built to carry heavy **cargo**. The rocket is called the Falcon Heavy. Today, it will make its first trip to space.

A Falcon Heavy rocket launches at the Kennedy Space Center in Florida.

The rocket's engines roar to life. They shoot out hot gases. The rocket zooms up into the air.

Pieces of the rocket come apart as it flies. First, the two rocket **boosters** use up their fuel. They fall away from the main rocket.

FUN FACT

The Falcon Heavy carried an electric car to space. A dummy named Starman rode in the car.

 After falling off the main rocket, the boosters fly back to the launch pad.

A few minutes later, the main rocket releases the upper **stage**. The rocket returns to the ground. But the upper stage keeps flying through space. It will travel around the sun.

CHAPTER 2

INTO SPACE

The first rockets were fireworks. They were invented hundreds of years ago in China. Robert Goddard built the first modern rocket in 1926. It used oxygen and gasoline to produce power.

 Robert Goddard designed several early rockets. This one launched in 1940.

Germany developed V-2 rockets during World War II (1939–1945).

Rockets first reached space in the 1940s. At this time, Germany began building rocket **missiles**. The Soviet Union and the United States studied these rockets. They tried to build their own. The Soviet Union sent a rocket to space in 1957.

RACE TO THE MOON

In the 1960s, the United States wanted to send a person to the moon. So did the Soviet Union. Each country wanted to be first. A US spacecraft landed on the moon in 1969. Saturn V rockets launched the US spacecraft.

The rocket released a **satellite**. This was the first object a rocket sent to space.

Another Soviet rocket carried a man to space in 1961. He became the first person to orbit Earth. The next year, the United States sent a person into orbit.

FUN FACT

A rocket launched the *Juno* spacecraft in 2011. The spacecraft reached Jupiter five years later.

 An orange rocket and two white boosters helped launch the space shuttles.

By the 2000s, rockets had many uses. They carried satellites and spacecraft. Rockets launched space shuttles, too. The shuttles carried **astronauts** and supplies to the International Space Station (ISS).

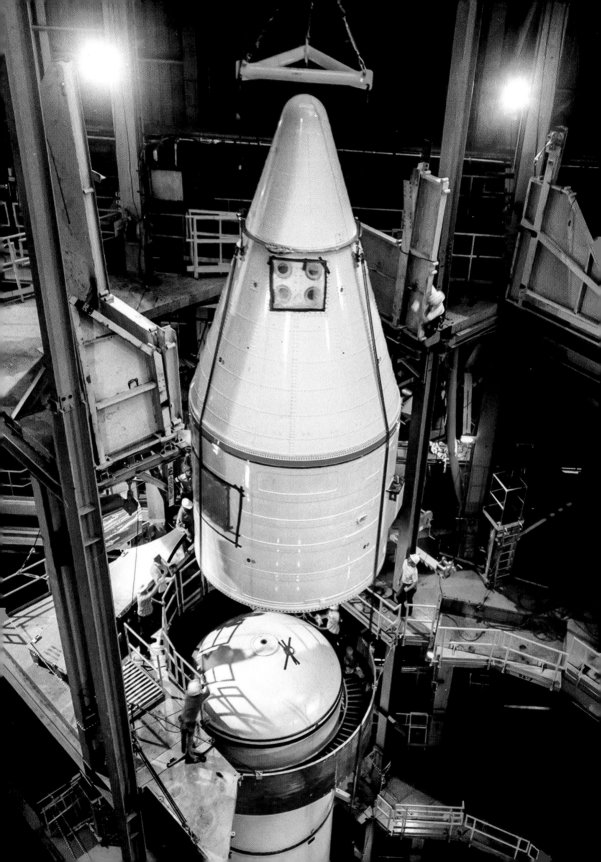

CHAPTER 3

MADE FOR FLIGHT

Rockets carry people and cargo to space. A rocket's cargo is also called its payload. The payload goes inside the rocket's nose cone. This part protects the payload until it reaches space.

 The nose cone is attached to the top of the rocket.

To reach space, rockets must escape the pull of Earth's **gravity**. They need lots of energy to do this. And they must go very fast. So, rockets have powerful engines.

In fact, the biggest part of a rocket is the **propulsion** system.

➤ ROCKET SPEED

Rockets reach very high speeds. They can go 25,000 miles per hour (40,000 km/h). That is 7 miles (11 km) every second. A rocket can travel to space in three minutes. If a car could drive to space, it would take 60 minutes.

 Zenit rockets like this one have carried several satellites to space.

This system includes the main

rocket and the rocket boosters.

Most boosters burn solid fuel. After they use up the fuel, the boosters fall off the rocket. That way, their weight does not slow the rocket as it travels.

A guidance system controls the rocket's flight. This system has many parts. It uses sensors,

FUN FACT

The Falcon Heavy has 27 engines. Together, they create as much power as 18 airplanes.

PARTS OF A ROCKET

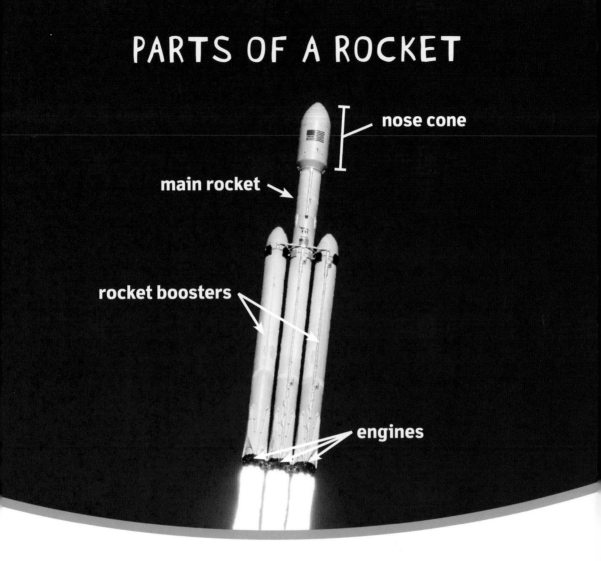

nose cone

main rocket

rocket boosters

engines

computers, and **radars**. All these
parts work together. They steer the
rocket. And they keep the rocket
steady as it flies.

ROCKET ENGINES

Engines burn fuel to produce power. An engine needs oxygen to burn fuel. However, there is no oxygen in space.

To solve this problem, rockets carry oxygen. Pumps send the oxygen and fuel to the combustion chamber. In this space, the oxygen and fuel mix together. The mixture is then burned to make a blast of hot gases. The gases shoot the rocket up off the ground. The rocket flies into the air. Then the gases shoot out the back of the rocket. They cause the rocket to move forward.

Nozzles at the bottom of the rocket shoot out hot gases.

CHAPTER 4

THE FUTURE OF ROCKETS

Rockets are very expensive. For many years, only governments could afford to build them. But that is beginning to change. A few private companies have started making rockets.

 Blue Origin is one company that has launched and landed a reusable rocket.

The first one was SpaceX. This company launched its first rocket in 2010. Since then, several other companies have launched rockets. They include Virgin Galactic and Blue Origin. Each company has its own design.

In most older rockets, the engines and boosters were used only once.

FUN FACT

A spaceship launched by a SpaceX rocket reached the ISS in 2012.

> The Skybolt 2 rocket is designed by a British
> company called Starchaser Industries.

Then these parts dropped off the
rocket. They burned up as they fell
back to Earth. Many newer rockets
have reusable parts. These parts
can be used over and over.

 Scientists on the ground help find and steer the parts of the rocket that fall back to Earth.

Some parts fall into the ocean. Boats pick them up. They bring the parts back to land to use again. Other parts fly back to the launch pad. They land there. Then they are used for other rockets. Using parts again is less expensive. In time, sending rockets to space may not cost as much.

VACATION IN SPACE

A few companies are designing rockets that will carry tourists. The rockets will take people on a short trip to space. The companies hope to make space travel more common. People will buy tickets to ride inside the rockets. They may even be able to visit the ISS.

FOCUS ON
ROCKETS

Write your answers on a separate piece of paper.

1. Write a paragraph describing how a rocket launches.

2. Do you think space travel will become common in the future? Why or why not?

3. Where were the first rockets invented?
    A. China
    B. the Soviet Union
    C. the United States

4. What might happen to the payload if a rocket's nose cone fell apart?
    A. The payload might be damaged during the flight.
    B. The payload might be mixed with the rocket's fuel.
    C. The payload would not be affected.

5. What does **afford** mean in this book?

*Rockets are very expensive. For many years, only governments could **afford** to build them.*

    A. to pay for something

    B. to break something

    C. to learn about something

6. What does **reusable** mean in this book?

*Many newer rockets have **reusable** parts. These parts can be used over and over.*

    A. only used once

    B. used many times

    C. easy to see through

Answer key on page 32.

GLOSSARY

astronauts
People who are trained to work or travel in space.

boosters
Small rockets added to the side of a large rocket to provide extra power.

cargo
Items carried by a vehicle from one place to another.

gravity
The natural force that pulls objects toward Earth.

missiles
Weapons that are fired or launched at a target.

propulsion
Used for moving a vehicle forward.

radars
Devices that send out radio waves for detecting and locating objects.

satellite
An object or vehicle that orbits a planet or moon, often to collect information.

stage
One of the several sections that make up a rocket. Each stage has its own fuel and engine. Only the upper stage carries the payload.

TO LEARN MORE

BOOKS

Baker, David, and Heather Kissock. *Rockets*. New York: AV2 by Weigl, 2018.

Lock, Deborah. *Rocket Science*. New York: DK Publishing, 2015.

Rowell, Rebecca. *Building Rockets*. Lake Elmo, MN: Focus Readers, 2018.

NOTE TO EDUCATORS

Visit **www.focusreaders.com** to find lesson plans, activities, links, and other resources related to this title.

INDEX

Answer Key: 1. Answers will vary; **2.** Answers will vary; **3.** A; **4.** A; **5.** A; **6.** B